ROW QUILTS
Longitudes & Latitudes™

Edited by Carolyn S. Vagts

Annie's®

Introduction

Quilts are constructed in sections. Usually, first the blocks are made; these are joined into rows and then the rows are sewn together to make the quilt top. Settings can be horizontal, vertical or diagonal. That doesn't mean you can't vary the typical construction. These 10 quilted projects are typical settings but with visual differences. It's amazing how twisting or turning a block can change the appearance of the finished quilt. Assembling in rows doesn't mean they have to align in both directions. Quilts are like all things creative—the possibilities are endless. As you page through this book, let the projects inspire you. Your colors, your fabric choices and your style are all you need to make a fantastic quilt happen.

We have everything from a traditional row quilt that tells a story and can be personalized, to one that incorporates border fabric and paper piecing with a second option, to quilts with optical illusions and everything in between. There are quick and easy quilts and more challenging projects to satisfy all skill levels. Here are the project patterns you've been looking for!

Table of Contents

Evening Blooms Bed Runner,
page 21

Quick Snaps

Design by Gina Gempesaw
Quilted by Carole Whaling

This quick-to-assemble vertical-row quilt is perfect for showcasing large-scale prints.

Specifications
Skill Level: Beginner
Quilt Size: 48" x 66"
Block Size: 9" x 7" finished
Number of Blocks: 43

Materials
- 14 or more fat eighths large-scale prints or 1¾ yards total assorted scraps
- ½ yard light orange tonal
- ½ yard yellow tonal
- ⅝ yard salmon tonal
- ⅝ yard orange-with-yellow dots
- 1⅜ yards red tonal
- Backing to size
- Batting to size
- Thread
- Basic sewing tools and supplies

Cutting

From large-scale prints:
- Cut 43 (5½" x 7½") A rectangles.

From light orange tonal:
- Cut 8 (1½" by fabric width) strips.
  Subcut strips into 20 each 1½" x 5½" B1 and 1½" x 9½" C1 strips.

From yellow tonal:
- Cut 6 (1½" by fabric width) strips.
  Subcut strips into 14 each 1½" x 5½" B3 and 1½" x 9½" C3 strips.
- Cut 1 (4" by fabric width) strip.
  Subcut strip into 2 (4" x 9½") D2 rectangles.

From salmon tonal:
- Cut 7 (1½" by fabric width) strips.
  Subcut strips into 16 each 1½" x 5½" B2 and 1½" x 9½" C2 strips.
- Cut 1 (4" by fabric width) strip.
  Subcut strip into 1 (4" x 9½") D1 rectangle.

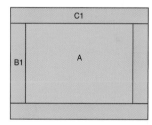

Quick Snap
9" x 7" Finished Block
Make 43

From orange-with-yellow dots:
- Cut 7 (1½" by fabric width) strips.
  Subcut strips into 16 each 1½" x 5½" B4 and 1½" x 9½" C4 strips.
- Cut 1 (4" by fabric width) strip.
  Subcut strip into 1 (4" x 9½") D3 rectangle.

From red tonal:
- Cut 8 (1½" by fabric width) strips.
  Subcut strips into 20 each 1½" x 5½" B5 and 1½" x 9½" C5 strips.
- Cut 6 (2" by fabric width) E/F strips.
- Cut 6 (2¼" by fabric width) binding strips.

Completing the Blocks

1. To complete one Quick Snap block, select one A rectangle and two each B1 and C1 strips.

2. Referring to Figure 1, sew B1 strips to opposite short ends of A and add the C1 strips to opposite long sides to complete the block; press seams toward B1 and C1 strips.

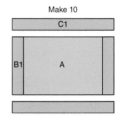

Make 10

Figure 1

3. Repeat steps 1 and 2 with remaining A rectangles and B and C strips, using same-fabric B and C strips for each block, to complete a total of 43 blocks referring to Figure 2 for number to make of each color.

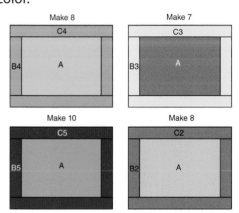

Make 8 — C4, B4, A

Make 7 — C3, B3, A

Make 10 — C5, B5, A

Make 8 — C2, B2, A

Figure 2

Completing the Quilt

The placement of the blocks in the vertical rows is important. They form a diagonal row of color when blocks are placed correctly. Refer to the Assembly Diagram for all row piecing.

1. Arrange and join nine Quick Snap blocks to make one vertical row; press. Repeat to make three rows.

2. Arrange and join eight Quick Snap blocks with two D rectangles to make a vertical row; press. Repeat to make a second row.

3. Arrange and join the vertical rows to complete the quilt center; press.

4. Join the E/F strips on the short ends to make a long strip; press. Subcut strip into two each 2" x 63½" E strips and 2" x 48½" F strips.

5. Sew E strips to opposite long sides and F strips to the top and bottom of the quilt center to complete the quilt top; press seams toward E and F strips.

6. Create a quilt sandwich referring to Finishing Your Quilt on page 55.

7. Quilt as desired.

8. Bind referring to Finishing Your Quilt on page 55 to finish. ∎

"I love large-scale prints, and this quilt shows a lot of them all at once. The warm colors used as the backgrounds make for a lively quilt." —Gina Gempesaw

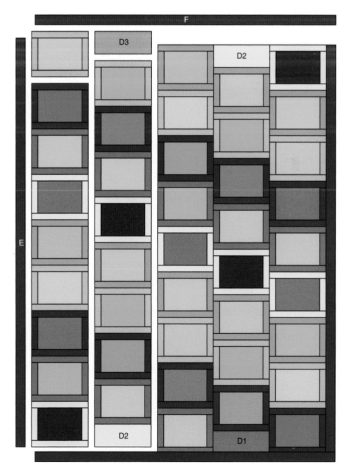

Quick Snaps
Assembly Diagram 48" x 66"

Abacus

Designed & Quilted by Julie Weaver

This quick and easy quilt in vertical rows would look wonderful in any color combination. Using precut 2½" strips will speed things up.

Specifications
Skill Level: Confident Beginner
Quilt Size: 51" x 60"
Block Sizes: 6" x 6" finished and 6" x 12" finished
Number of Blocks: 35 and 5

Materials
- ½ yard red-and-white chevron print
- 1 yard red tonal
- 1 yard light gray tonal
- 1⅓ yards black-with-white dots
- 1⅞ yards medium gray tonal
- Backing to size
- Batting to size
- Thread
- Basic sewing tools and supplies

Cutting

From red-and-white chevron print:
- Cut 5 (2½" by fabric width) B strips.

From red tonal:
- Cut 10 (2½" by fabric width) A strips.

From light gray tonal:
- Cut 16 (1½" by fabric width) G strips.

From black-with-white dots:
- Cut 4 (2½" by fabric width) E strips.
- Cut 8 (1½" by fabric width) F strips.
- Cut 6 (2¼" by fabric width) binding strips.

From medium gray tonal:
- Cut 7 (2½" by fabric width) strips.
  Subcut strips into 100 (2½") C squares.
- Cut 8 (2½" by fabric width) D strips.
- Cut 3 (2" by fabric width) H strips.
- Cut 3 (3½" by fabric width) I strips.

Completing the Bead Blocks
1. Sew a B strip between two A strips with right sides together along length to make an A-B strip set; press seams toward A. Repeat to make a total of five A-B strip sets.

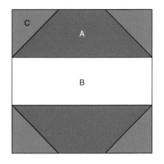

Bead
6 x 6" Finished Block
Make 25

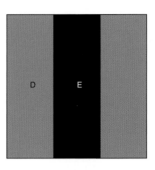

Rod Square
6 x 6" Finished Block
Make 10

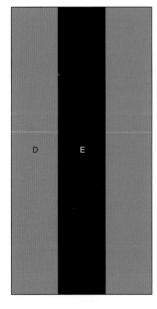

Rod Rectangle
6 x 12" Finished Block
Make 5

2. Subcut the A-B strip sets into 25 (6½" x 6½") square A-B units as shown in Figure 1.

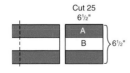

Cut 25
6½"

6½"

Figure 1

8

3. Mark a diagonal line from corner to corner on the wrong side of each C square.

4. Referring to Figure 2, place a C square right sides together on one corner of one A-B unit and stitch on the marked line; trim seam allowance to ¼" and press C to the right side.

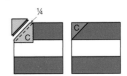

Figure 2

5. Repeat step 4 on each remaining corner of the A-B unit to complete one Bead block as shown in Figure 3.

Figure 3

6. Repeat steps 4 and 5 to complete a total of 25 Bead blocks.

Completing the Rod Blocks

1. Sew an E strip between two D strips with right sides together along length to make a D-E strip set; press seams toward E. Repeat to make a total of four D-E strip sets.

2. Subcut the D-E strip sets into 10 (6½" x 6½") Rod Square blocks and five 12½" x 6½" Rod Rectangle blocks referring to Figure 4.

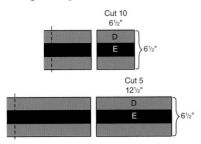

Figure 4

Completing the Quilt

1. Join the F strips on the short ends to make a long strip; press.

2. Repeat step 1 with G strips, joining eight strips to make two G strips.

3. Sew a G strip to opposite long edges of the F strip to make an F-G strip set; press seams toward F. Subcut the F-G strip set into six 3½" x 54½" F-G strips.

4. Arrange and join the Bead, Rod Square and Rod Rectangle blocks to make five vertical rows referring to the Assembly Diagram for positioning of blocks; press seams away from the Bead blocks.

5. Arrange and join the F-G strips with the vertical block rows to complete the quilt center; press seams toward the F-G strips.

6. Join the H strips on the short ends to make a long strip; press. Subcut strip into two 2" x 54½" H strips. Sew these strips to opposite long sides of the quilt center; press seams toward the G strips.

7. Join the I strips on the short ends to make a long strip; press. Subcut strip into two 3½" x 51½" I strips. Sew these strips to the top and bottom of the pieced center to complete the quilt top; press seams toward the I strips.

8. Create a quilt sandwich referring to Finishing Your Quilt on page 55.

9. Quilt as desired.

10. Bind referring to Finishing Your Quilt on page 55 to finish. ■

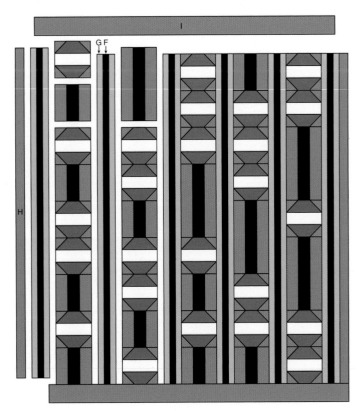

Abacus
Assembly Diagram 51" x 60"

"I try to take 'inspiration breaks' on a regular basis to see what's new in fabric at the quilt shops and in home decor at the department stores. On one of my last trips out (I get a lot of inspiration on the Internet too), I saw chevrons in all colors and lots of black and gray fabrics. The challenge of using the chevron, black and gray fabrics was the inspiration for this quilt. I knew I wanted something simple and geometric, and this quilt was born!" —Julie Weaver

Stardom

Designed & Quilted by Wendy Sheppard

Part of the fun of working with a row quilt pattern is the secondary patterns that can appear. Fabric color and placement in this quilt creates a diagonal pattern even though it's assembled horizontally.

Specifications

Skill Level: Advanced
Quilt Size: 51" x 69"
Block Size: 8" x 8" finished
Number of Blocks: 35

Materials

- 1 fat quarter black-with-gold metallic
- ⅝ yard black music print
- ⅝ yard yellow metallic
- ⅝ gray musical instruments print
- ⅝ yard cream composer print
- ⅔ yard white music score print
- 1¼ yards pumpkin solid
- 2⅓ yards white tonal
- Backing to size
- Batting to size
- Thread
- Basic sewing tools and supplies

Cutting

From black-with-gold metallic:

- Cut 1 (1½" x 21") strip.
    Subcut strip into 12 (1½") I squares.

From black music print:

- Cut 1 (9¼" by fabric width) strip.
    Subcut strip into 4 (9¼") squares. Cut each square on both diagonals to make 16 G1 triangles; set aside 2 triangles for another project.
- Cut 3 (2½" by fabric width) strips.
    Subcut strips into 16 (2½") E1 squares and 16 (2½" x 4½") D1 rectangles.
- Cut 1 (9¼" by fabric width) strip.
    Subcut strip into 4 (9¼") squares. Cut each square on both diagonals to make 16 G1 triangles; set aside 2 triangles for another project.

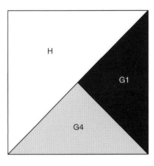

Corner 1
8" x 8" Finished Block
Make 2

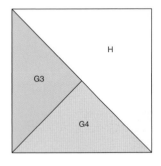

Corner 2
8" x 8" Finished Block
Make 2

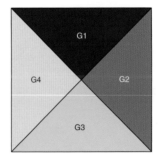

Triangles
8" x 8" Finished Block
Make 14 total in different versions

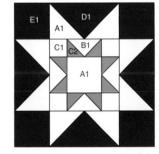

Star-in-a-Star
8" x 8" Finished Block
Make 17 total in different versions

From yellow metallic:

- Cut 1 (9¼" by fabric width) strip.
    Subcut strip into 4 (9¼") squares. Cut each square on both diagonals to make 16 G3 triangles; set aside 2 triangles for another project.
- Cut 3 (2½" by fabric width) strips.
    Subcut strips into 16 (2½") E2 squares and 16 (2½" x 4½") D2 rectangles.

From gray musical instruments print:
- Cut 1 (9¼" by fabric width) strip.
  Subcut strip into 4 (9¼") squares. Cut each square on both diagonals to make 16 G2 triangles; set aside 2 triangles for another project.
- Cut 3 (2½" by fabric width) strips.
  Subcut strips into 16 (2½") E3 squares and 16 (2½" x 4½") D3 rectangles.

From cream composer print:
- Cut 6 (3" by fabric width) L/M strips.

From white music score print:
- Cut 1 (9¼" by fabric width) strip.
  Subcut strip into 4 (9¼") squares. Cut each square on both diagonals to make 16 G4 triangles.
- Cut 4 (2½" by fabric width) strips.
  Subcut strips into 20 (2½") E4 squares and 20 (2½" x 4½") D4 rectangles.

From pumpkin solid:
- Cut 7 (1½" by fabric width) strips.
  Subcut strips into 132 (1½") C2 squares and 16 (1½" x 2½") B2 rectangles.
- Cut 3 (2½" by fabric width) strips.
  Subcut strips into 38 (2½") A2 squares.
- Cut 7 (2¼" by fabric width) binding strips.

From white tonal:
- Cut 1 (9¼" by fabric width) strip.
  Subcut strip into 2 (9¼") squares. Cut each square on both diagonals to make 8 F triangles; set aside 2 triangles for another project.
  Subcut remainder of strip into 2 (8⅞") squares. Cut each square in half on 1 diagonal to make 4 H triangles.
- Cut 7 (1½" by fabric width) strips.
  Subcut strips into 96 (1½") C1 squares and 52 (1½" x 2½") B1 rectangles.
- Cut 8 (2½" by fabric width) strips.
  Subcut strips into 115 (2½") A1 squares.
- Cut 3 (8½" by fabric width) strips.
  Subcut strips into 72 (1½" x 8½") J sashing strips.
- Cut 3 (1½" by fabric width) K strips.

Completing the Star Blocks

There are six versions of the Star-in-a-Star block. Refer to Figures 8 and 9 for positioning of pieces in each version.

1. Select the following to make one Star-in-a-Star Version 1 block: nine A1 and eight C2 squares, four each C1 and E1 squares, and four each B1 and D1 rectangles.

2. Set aside one A1 square for the center. Draw a diagonal line from corner to corner on the wrong side of the remaining eight A1 squares and the C2 squares.

3. Referring to Figure 1, place a C2 square right sides together on one end of a B1 rectangle and stitch on the marked line; trim seam to ¼" and press C2 to the right side. Repeat on the opposite end of B1 to complete one B-C unit. Repeat to make four B-C units.

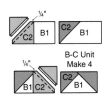

Figure 1

4. Repeat step 3 with A1 and D1 pieces to make four A-D units referring to Figure 2.

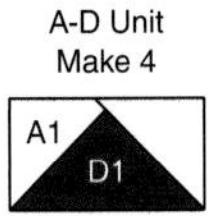

Figure 2

5. Sew a B-C unit to opposite sides of the remaining A1 square as shown in Figure 3; press seams toward A.

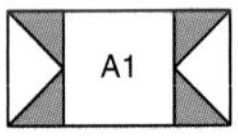

Figure 3

6. Sew a C1 square to opposite ends of each of the remaining B-C units to make a row as shown in Figure 4; press seams toward C1. Repeat to make a second row.

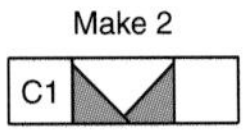

Figure 4

7. Join the pieced rows to complete the block center referring to Figure 5; press seams away from the center row.

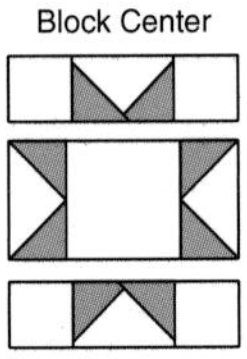

Figure 5

8. Sew an A-D unit to opposite sides of the block center to complete the center row referring to Figure 6; press seams away from the block center.

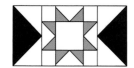

Figure 6

9. Sew an E1 square to each end of each remaining A-D unit to make the top row as shown in Figure 7; press seams toward the E1 squares. Repeat to make the bottom row.

Make 2

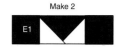

Figure 7

10. Sew the center row between the top and bottom rows to complete one Star-in-a-Star Version 1 block referring to Figure 8; press seams away from the center row.

Version 1
Make 4

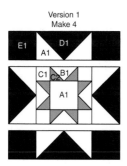

Figure 8

11. Repeat steps 1–10 to complete a total of four Star-in-a-Star Version 1 blocks.

12. Repeat steps 1–10 substituting different numbered A, B, C, D and E pieces for each version of the block referring to Figure 9 for pieces used, placement of pieces and number of each version to make.

Completing the Triangles Blocks

There are five versions of the Triangles blocks. Refer to drawings for positioning of pieces in each version.

1. To complete one Triangles 1 block, select one each F, G1, G2 and G3 triangle.

2. Sew a G3 triangle to a G2 triangle on a short edge and a G1 triangle to an F triangle on a short edge referring to Figure 10. Press seams toward G1 and G3.

Figure 10

3. Join the two pieced triangle units to complete one Triangles 1 block referring to Figure 11; press seam open.

Triangles 1
Make 2

Figure 11

4. Repeat steps 1–3 to complete a second Triangles 1 block.

5. Repeat steps 1–3 to complete two each Triangles blocks 2, 3 and 4, and six Triangles 5 blocks referring to Figure 12 for pieces to use and positioning.

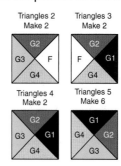

Figure 12

Version 2
Make 2

Version 3
Make 2

Version 4
Make 4

Version 5
Make 4

Version 6
Make 1

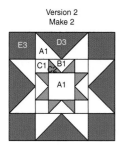 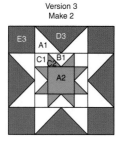 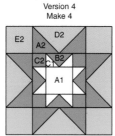 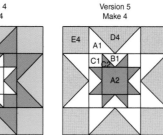 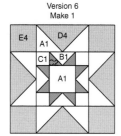

Figure 9

14

Completing the Corner Blocks

1. To complete one Corner 1 block, select one each G1, G4 and H triangle.

2. Sew the G1 triangle to the G4 triangle on one short side as shown in Figure 13; press seam toward G1.

Figure 13

3. Sew the H triangle to the long edge of the pieced G unit to complete one Corner 1 block referring to Figure 14; press seam toward H.

Make 2

Figure 14

4. Repeat steps 1–3 to complete a second black notes Corner 1 block.

5. Repeat steps 1–3 to complete two Corner 2 blocks referring to Figure 15.

Make 2

Figure 15

Completing the Quilt

1. Arrange and join the Star-in-a-Star blocks with the Triangles blocks and J sashing strips in five rows of five blocks and six J strips each, referring to the Assembly Diagram for positioning of blocks in rows; press seams toward J strips. Repeat for top and bottom rows, using one each Corner 1 and 2 blocks, one Triangles block and two Star-in-a-Star blocks in each row as shown in Assembly Diagram.

2. Arrange and join five J strips with two each C1, C2 and I squares to make a sashing row referring to the Assembly Diagram for positioning of the squares; press seams toward J. Repeat to make a total of six sashing rows.

> ### Here's a Tip
>
> *There are many block variations used in this quilt. Placement of the triangles in the Triangles blocks forms a secondary design when placement is correct and the fabrics have enough contrast to differentiate between them. For example, the black/gray diagonal pattern would not be so prominent if the fabrics used did not contrast with the white/yellow fabrics used to form the second diagonal design. Careful placement of blocks and units when blocks are stitched is very important to create the design in this music-themed quilt.*

Stardom
Assembly Diagram 51" x 69"

3. Arrange and join the block rows and the sashing rows to complete the quilt center referring to the Assembly Diagram for positioning of all rows to create the secondary design; press seams toward the sashing rows.

4. Join the K strips on the short ends to make a long strip; press. Subcut strip into two 1½" x 46½" K strips.

5. Sew the K strips to the top and bottom of the quilt center; press seams toward strips.

6. Join the L/M strips on the short ends to make a long strip; press. Subcut strip into two each 3" x 64½" L strips and 3" x 51½" M strips.

7. Sew L strips to opposite long sides and M strips to the top and bottom of the quilt center to complete the quilt top; press.

8. Create a quilt sandwich referring to Finishing Your Quilt on page 55.

9. Quilt as desired.

10. Bind referring to Finishing Your Quilt on page 55 to finish. ∎

Hanging by a Chain

Design by Nancy Scott
Quilted by Masterpiece Quilting

This quilt is pieced into vertical rows by setting the blocks on point and adding setting triangles.

Specifications
Skill Level: Intermediate
Quilt Size: 105" x 105"
Block Size: 12" x 12" finished
Number of Blocks: 27

Materials
- 2⅔ yards aqua tonal
- 4¾ yards purple tonal
- 4¾ yards cream solid
- Backing to size
- Batting to size
- Thread
- Spray starch (optional)
- Basic sewing tools and supplies

Cutting

From aqua tonal:
- Cut 27 (2½" by fabric width) A/D/F strips.
- Cut 4 (4½" by fabric width) strips.
  Subcut strips into 54 (2½" x 4½") G rectangles.

From purple tonal:
- Cut 11 (2½" by fabric width) B strips.
- Cut 11 (2¼" by fabric width) binding strips.
- Use remaining fabric length to cut the following border strips: Cut 2 each 10½" x 85½" J strips and 10½" x 105½" K strips.

From cream solid:
- Cut 16 (2½" by fabric width) C/E strips.
- Cut 6 (18¼" by fabric width) strips.
  Subcut strips into 11 (18¼") squares and 2 (9⅜") squares. Cut each 18¼" square on both diagonals to make 44 H triangles.
- Cut 1 (9⅜" by fabric width) strip.
  Subcut strip into 4 (9⅜") squares. Cut each square and the 2 cut above in half on 1 diagonal to make 12 I triangles.

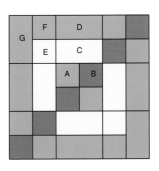

Chain
12" x 12" Finished Block
Make 27

Completing the Chain Blocks
1. Sew an A strip to a B strip along length to make an A-B strip set; press seam toward B. Repeat to make a total of 11 A-B strip sets.

2. Subcut the A-B strip sets into 162 (2½" x 4½") A-B segments as shown in Figure 1.

A-B Segments
Cut 162

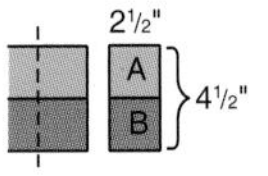

2½"

A
B } 4½"

Figure 1

3. Join two A-B segments to make a Four-Patch unit as shown in Figure 2; press. Repeat to make a total of 81 Four-Patch units.

Four-Patch Unit
Make 81

Figure 2

4. Sew a C strip to a D strip along length to make a C-D strip set; press seam toward D. Repeat to make a total of 12 C-D strip sets.

5. Subcut the C-D strip sets into 108 (4½" x 4½") side units as shown in Figure 3.

Side Units
Cut 108
4½"

Figure 3

6. Sew an E strip to an F strip to make an E-F strip set; press seam toward E. Repeat to make a total of four E-F strip sets.

7. Subcut the E-F strip sets into 54 (2½" x 4½") E-F segments as shown in Figure 4.

E-F Segments
Cut 54
2½"

Figure 4

8. Sew a G rectangle to an E-F segment to make a corner unit as shown in Figure 5; press seam toward G. Repeat to make a total of 54 corner units.

Corner Unit
Make 54

Figure 5

9. To complete one Chain block, select three Four-Patch units, four side units and two corner units.

10. Sew a side unit to opposite sides of one Four-Patch unit to make the center row referring to Figure 6; press seams toward the side units.

Make 1

Figure 6

11. Sew a corner unit to one end and a Four-Patch unit to the opposite end of a side unit to make the top row referring to Figure 7 for positioning of units; press seams toward the side unit. Repeat to make the bottom row.

Make 2

Figure 7

12. Sew the top and bottom rows to the center row to complete one Chain block referring to Figure 8; press seams away from the center row.

Figure 8

13. Repeat steps 9–12 to complete a total of 27 Chain blocks.

Completing the Quilt

1. Select four Chain blocks, and referring to Working With Bias Edges on page 19, cut on the diagonal to make four half-blocks. *Note: Place the leftover section of the trimmed blocks in your scrap basket for use in a future project.*

2. Arrange and join the blocks and half-blocks in five vertical rows with the H and I triangles referring to the Assembly Diagram for positioning of blocks in the rows; press seams away from the blocks.

3. Join the rows as pieced, again referring to the Assembly Diagram for positioning, to complete the quilt center; press.

4. Sew J strips to the top and bottom, and K strips to opposite sides to complete the quilt top; press seams toward strips.

5. Create a quilt sandwich referring to Finishing Your Quilt on page 55.

6. Quilt as desired.

7. Bind referring to Finishing Your Quilt on page 55 to finish. ■

"The vertical row layout is one I've seen used on vintage quilts, and each time I see it, I love it more and more. The fresh colors in this quilt and their placement within the block really add a contemporary look." —Nancy Scott

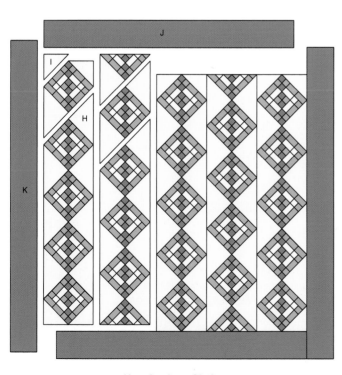

Hanging by a Chain
Assembly Diagram 105" x 105"

Working With Bias Edges

When cutting blocks on the diagonal to make half-blocks, there are bias edges that will stretch if care is not taken to stabilize them.

To reduce the stretch, apply spray starch to the wrong side of the diagonal area of the block to be cut; let dry.

Draw a line across the diagonal of the wrong side of the block and staystitch ⅛" from the line on the side to be trimmed as shown in Figure A.

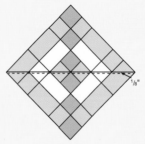

Figure A

Cut the block ¼" from the marked line as shown in Figure B. Note that the fabric at each end will not fill the seam allowance when stitching the half-block together with other pieces as shown in Figure C.

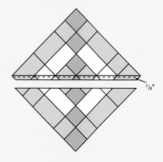

Figure B

Figure C

Evening Blooms Bed Runner

Designed & Quilted by Julie Weaver

Turn basic blocks into a stunning bed runner row by row. You'll be amazed just how easy it is to make this beauty.

Specifications

Skill Level: Confident Beginner
Quilt Size: 72" x 32"
Block Sizes: 9" x 9" finished and 6" x 6" finished
Number of Blocks: 6 and 18

Materials

- ¼ yard light yellow print
- ¼ yard dark gray solid
- ½ yard black floral
- ½ yard black-and-white stripe
- ½ yard dark yellow print
- ¾ yard black-with-white dots
- ⅞ yard black solid
- 1 yard light gray solid
- Backing to size
- Batting to size
- Thread
- Basic sewing tools and supplies

Cutting

From light yellow print:
- Cut 2 (2" by fabric width) A1 strips.

From dark gray solid:
- Cut 3 (2" by fabric width) B2 strips.

From black floral:
- Cut 2 (3½" by fabric width) strips.
  Subcut strips into 20 (3½") C squares.
- Cut 1 (6½" by fabric width) strip.
  Subcut strip into 10 (3½" x 6½") E rectangles.

From black-and-white stripe:
- Cut 2 (7" by fabric width) strips.
  Subcut strips into 2 (7" x 32½") N strips.

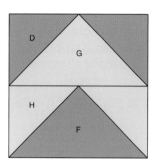

Yellow Chevron
6" x 6" Finished Block
Make 8

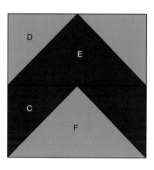

Black Chevron
6" x 6" Finished Block
Make 10

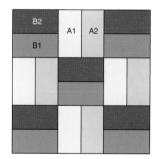

Evening Blooms
9" x 9" Finished Block
Make 6

From dark yellow print:
- Cut 2 (2" by fabric width) A2 strips.
- Cut 1 (6½" by fabric width) strip.
  Subcut strip into 8 (3½" x 6½") G rectangles
  and 4 (3½") H squares.
- Cut 1 (3½" by fabric width) strip.
  Subcut strip into 12 (3½") H squares
  (to total 16 H squares).

From black-with-white dots:
• Cut 10 (2" by fabric width) I/J/L strips.

From black solid:
• Cut 5 (1½" by fabric width) K/M strips.
• Cut 6 (2¼" by fabric width) binding strips.

From light gray solid:
• Cut 3 (2" by fabric width) B1 strips.
• Cut 2 (6½" by fabric width) strips.
  Subcut strips into 18 (3½" x 6½") F rectangles.
• Cut 3 (3½" by fabric width) strips.
  Subcut strips into 36 (3½") D squares.

Completing the Evening Blooms Blocks

1. Sew an A1 strip to an A2 strip with right sides together along the length to make an A strip set; press seam to one side. Repeat to make a second strip set.

2. Subcut the A strip sets into 24 (3½" x 3½") A units as shown in Figure 1.

Cut 24
3½"

A1
A2

}3½"

Figure 1

3. Repeat steps 1 and 2 with B1 and B2 strips to make three strip sets and cut 30 (3½" x 3½") B units referring to Figure 2.

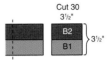

Cut 30
3½"

B2
B1

}3½"

Figure 2

4. Select four A units and five B units to complete one Evening Blossom block.

5. Sew an A unit between two B units to make the top row referring to Figure 3; press seams toward the A unit. Repeat to make the bottom row.

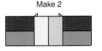

Make 2

Figure 3

6. Sew a B unit between two A units to make the center row referring to Figure 4; press seams toward the A units.

Figure 4

7. Sew the center row between the top and bottom rows referring to Figure 5 to complete one block; press seams away from the center row.

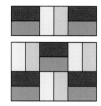

Figure 5

8. Repeat steps 4–7 to complete a total of six Evening Blooms blocks.

Completing the Chevron Blocks

1. Draw a diagonal line from corner to corner on the wrong side of each C, D and H square.

2. To complete one Black Chevron block, select one each E and F rectangle, and two each C and D squares.

3. Referring to Figure 6, place a D square right sides together on one corner of E and stitch on the marked line referring to Figure 6; trim seam allowance to ¼" and press D to the right side.

Figure 6

4. Repeat step 3 on the opposite corner of E to complete the D-E unit as shown in Figure 7.

Figure 7

5. Repeat steps 3 and 4 with two C squares and one F rectangle to make a C-F unit referring to Figure 8.

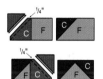

Figure 8

6. Sew the C-F unit to the D-E unit as shown in Figure 9 to complete one Black Chevron block; press seam toward the D-E unit.

Figure 9

7. Repeat steps 2–6 to complete a total of 10 Black Chevron blocks.

8. Repeat steps 2–6 with F rectangles and H squares, and G rectangles and D squares referring to Figure 10 to make a total of eight Yellow Chevron blocks.

Figure 10

Completing the Bed Runner

1. Arrange and join the Evening Blooms blocks to make the center row referring to the Assembly Diagram for positioning of blocks; press seams in one direction.

2. Join four Yellow Chevron blocks and five Black Chevron blocks to make the top row, again referring to the Assembly Diagram for positioning of blocks; press seams in one direction. Repeat to make the bottom row.

3. Join the I/J/L strips on the short ends to make a long strip; press. Subcut the strip into four 2" x 54½" I strips, two 2" x 27½" J strips and two 2" x 57½" L strips.

4. Join the center, top and bottom rows with the I strips beginning and ending with I strips to complete the runner center; press seams toward strips.

5. Sew a J strip to opposite ends of the runner center; press seams toward strips.

6. Join the K/M strips on the short ends to make a long strip; press. Subcut strip into two 1½" x 57½" K strips and two 1½" x 32½" M strips.

7. Sew K strips to opposite long sides of the runner center; press seams toward K strips.

8. Sew L strips to opposite long sides and M strips to the short ends of the runner center; press seams toward L and M strips.

9. Sew N strips to the short ends of the runner center to complete the bed runner top; press seams toward N strips.

10. Create a quilt sandwich referring to Finishing Your Quilt on page 55.

11. Quilt as desired.

12. Bind referring to Finishing Your Quilt on page 55 to finish. ∎

Here's a Tip

Pin the Chevron blocks together at the center seam junctions to make the Chevron seams align.

"I like the chevron design I am seeing on just about everything when I go on my inspiration excursions. In the quilting world, the chevrons are just half-square triangles or Flying Geese units. Since I prefer making Flying Geese units, I decided to use them to make my chevrons. I guess you could say chevrons were my inspiration for this quilt. I am also drawn to blocks that look like they're woven, so basically the choice of blocks was my inspiration." —Julie Weaver

Evening Blooms Bed Runner
Assembly Diagram 72" x 32"

Ribbon Play

Designed & Quilted by Robin Waggoner

This vertical row construction, easy piecing and careful color placement will net you a faux-dimensional finish.

Specifications

Skill Level: Intermediate
Quilt Size: 78" x 104"
Block Size: 12" x 12" finished
Number of Blocks: 40

Materials

- ³⁄₈ yard each 5 dark tonals: teal, green, purple, orange and pink
- ½ yard each 5 light tonals: teal, green, purple, orange and pink
- 1⅝ yards blue tonal
- 1⅔ yards brown tonal
- 3⅔ yards white tonal
- Backing to size
- Batting to size
- Thread
- Rotary ruler with a 45-degree angle line
- Basic sewing tools and supplies

Cutting

From each dark tonal:
- Cut 1 (4½" by fabric width) strip.
    Subcut strips into 2 (4½" x 12⅞")
      B rectangles each fabric.
- Cut 1 (4⅞" by fabric width) strip.
    Subcut strip into 7 (4⅞") squares.
      Cut each square in half on 1 diagonal
      to make 14 E triangles each fabric.

From each light tonal:
- Cut 1 (12⅞" by fabric width) strip.
    Subcut strip into 3 (12⅞") squares.
      Cut each square in half on 1 diagonal
      to make 6 F triangles each fabric.

From blue tonal:
- Cut 9 (2½" by fabric width) L/M strips.
- Cut 9 (2¼" by fabric width) binding strips.

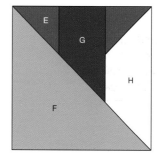

Ribbon Play
12" x 12" Finished Block
Make 30

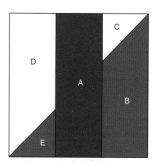

Ribbon End
12" x 12" Finished Block
Make 10

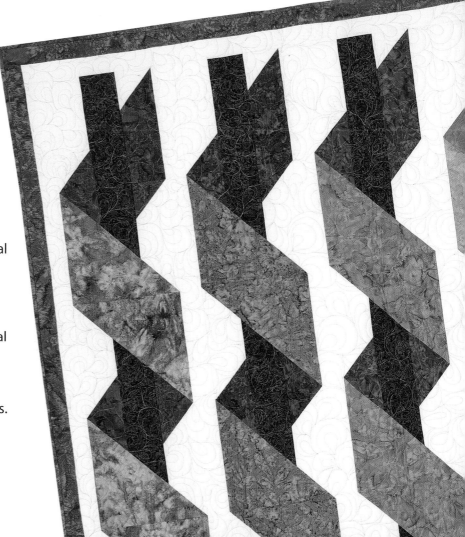

From brown tonal:
- Cut 11 (4½" by fabric width) strips.
  Subcut strips into 10 (4½" x 12½") A rectangles and 30 (4½" x 8⅞") G rectangles.

From white tonal:
- Cut 10 (3" by fabric width) I strips.
- Cut 9 (2½" by fabric width) J/K strips.
- Cut 10 (4½" by fabric width) strips.
  Subcut strips into 30 (4½" x 13¼") H rectangles.
- Cut 4 (4½" by fabric width) strips.
  Subcut strips into 10 (4½" x 12⅞") D rectangles.
- Cut 1 (4⅞" by fabric width) strip.
  Subcut strip into 5 (4⅞") squares. Cut each square in half on 1 diagonal to make 10 C triangles.

Completing the Ribbon Play Blocks

1. Trim the G and H rectangles referring to the Trimming Angled Pieces sidebar on page 29.

2. To complete one Ribbon Play block, select one each G and H piece, and one F triangle and two E triangles from the same color family.

3. Sew E to one angled end of H to make an H-E unit as shown in Figure 1; press seam toward E.

Figure 1

4. Sew G to the E-H unit and add another E to make a half-block as shown in Figure 2; press seams toward G.

Figure 2

5. Sew F to the half-block to complete one Ribbon Play block; press seam toward F.

6. Repeat steps 2–5 to complete six Ribbon Play blocks in each color family referring to Figure 3.

Make 6 each

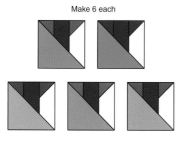

Figure 3

Completing the Ribbon End Blocks

1. Trim the B and D rectangles referring to the Trimming Angled Pieces sidebar on page 29.

2. To complete one Ribbon End block select one each A rectangle and C and D piece, and one each B piece and E triangle from the same color family.

3. Sew C to B and E to D as shown in Figure 4; press seams toward B and D.

Figure 4

4. Join the two pieced units with A referring to Figure 5 to complete one block; press seams toward A.

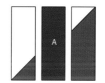

Figure 5

5. Repeat steps 2–4 to complete a total of two end blocks in each color family referring to Figure 6.

Make 2 each

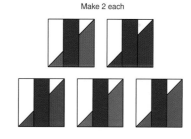

Figure 6

Completing the Quilt

1. Join the I strips on the short ends to make a long strip; press. Subcut strips into four 3" x 96½" I strips.

2. Arrange and join six Ribbon Play blocks of one color family and add a matching Ribbon End block to each end of the strip to make a vertical row referring to the Assembly Diagram; press seams in one direction. Repeat to make five vertical rows—one of each color family.

3. Join the vertical rows with the I strips; press seams toward the strips.

4. Join the J/K strips on the short ends to make a long strip; press. Subcut strip into two each 2½" x 96½" J strips and 2½" x 74½" K strips. Sew the J strips to opposite long sides and K strips to the top and bottom of the quilt center; press seams toward J and K strips.

5. Repeat step 4 with the L/M strips to cut two each 2½" x 100½" L strips and 2½" x 78½" M strips. Sew L strips to opposite long sides and M strips to the top and bottom of the quilt center to complete the quilt top; press seams toward L and M strips.

6. Create a quilt sandwich referring to Finishing Your Quilt on page 55.

7. Quilt as desired.

8. Bind referring to Finishing Your Quilt on page 55 to finish. ■

"This quilt makes me feel like spring with the colors of a blooming garden. It was inspired by the notion of a Maypole." —Robin Waggoner

Ribbon Play Alternate Size
Assembly Diagram 63½" x 80"
Make a lap-size quilt by making only
4 rows with 6 blocks in each row

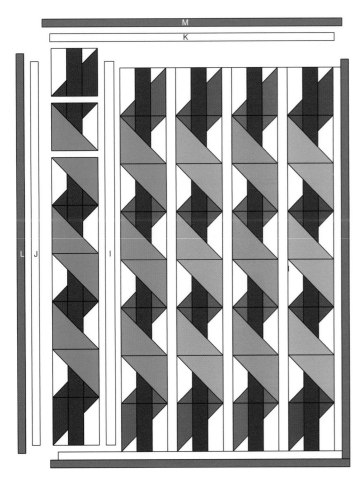

Ribbon Play
Assembly Diagram 78" x 104"

Trimming Angled Pieces

To avoid the use of templates, trim the angles on the B, D, G and H pieces using the 45-degree–angle line on a rotary ruler.

1. To trim, cut the B, D, G and H pieces to the sizes given in the cutting list.

2. Select the B rectangle and place horizontally right side up on a flat surface.

3. Align the 45-degree line on the ruler on the top edge of the strip and the edge of the ruler exactly intersecting the right bottom corner of B; cut as shown in Figure A.

45-degree–angle line

B

Figure A

4. Repeat steps 2 and 3 with remaining B rectangles and D rectangles.

5. Repeat steps 2 and 3 with G rectangles except make the cut on the left end of the strip as shown in Figure B.

G

Figure B

6. Repeat steps 2 and 3 with H rectangles except cut the angle on both ends as shown in Figure C.

H

Figure C

English Garden Runner

Design by Gina Gempesaw
Quilted by Carole Whaling

Turn Drunkard's Path and quarter-square Triangles blocks into this blooming beauty by setting them on the diagonal.

Specifications
Skill Level: Intermediate
Runner Size: 59⅜" x 19¾"
Block Size: 7" x 7" finished
Number of Blocks: 24

Materials
- ⅞ yard red tonal
- 1 yard orange floral
- 1⅝ yards cream tonal
- Backing to size
- Batting to size
- Thread
- Template material
- Basic sewing tools and supplies

Cutting
Prepare templates for A and B pieces using patterns given in the pattern insert. Cut as directed on each pattern.

From red tonal:
- Cut 1 (8¼" by fabric width) strip.
  Subcut strip into 2 (8¼") squares; cut the squares on both diagonals to make 8 C2 triangles.

From orange floral:
- Cut 1 (7½" by fabric width) strip.
  Subcut strip into 5 (7½") D squares.
- Cut 1 (8¼" by fabric width) strip.
  Subcut strip into 1 (8¼") square; cut the square on both diagonals to make 4 C1 triangles.

From cream tonal:
- Cut 1 (8¼" by fabric width) strip.
  Subcut strip into 1 (8¼") C3 square and 2 (5⅞") E squares. Cut the C3 square on both diagonals to make 4 C3 triangles. Cut the E squares in half on 1 diagonal to make 4 E triangles.
- Cut 5 (2¼" by fabric width) binding strips.

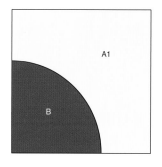

Cream Drunkard's Path
7" x 7" Finished Block
Make 12

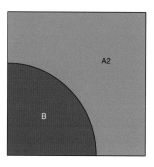

Orange Drunkard's Path
7" x 7" Finished Block
Make 8

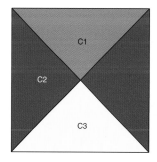

Triangles
7" x 7" Finished Block
Make 4

Completing the Drunkard's Path Blocks
1. To complete one Cream Drunkard's Path block, select one each A1 and B piece.

2. Referring to the Cream Drunkard's Path block drawing and to Curved Piecing on page 33, sew B to A1 to complete one block.

3. Repeat steps 1 and 2 to make a total of 12 Cream Drunkard's Path blocks.

4. Referring to the Orange Drunkard's Path block drawing, repeat steps 1 and 2 with A2 and B pieces to complete a total of eight Orange Drunkard's Path blocks.

Completing the Triangles Blocks

1. Select one each C1 and C3 triangle and two C2 triangles to complete one Triangles block.

2. Arrange and join one each C2 and C3 triangle on the short sides to make a C2-C3 unit referring to Figure 1; press seam toward C2. Repeat with C2 and C1 triangles to make a C1-C2 unit, again referring to Figure 1; press seam toward C2.

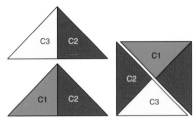

Figure 1

3. Join the two pieced units, again referring to Figure 1, to complete one block; press.

4. Repeat steps 1–3 to complete a total of four Triangles blocks.

Completing the Runner

1. Arrange and join the pieced blocks with the D squares in diagonal rows referring to Figure 2; press seams toward D squares.

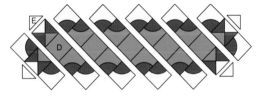

Figure 2

2. Add an E triangle to each C3 edge, again referring to Figure 2; press seams toward E.

3. Join the diagonal rows to complete the runner center. Using a straightedge, trim excess A1 pieces around the outer edge at the edge of the seam allowance to square up the runner as shown in Figure 3.

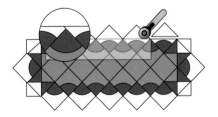

Figure 3

4. Create a quilt sandwich referring to Finishing Your Quilt on page 55.

5. Quilt as desired.

6. Bind referring to Finishing Your Quilt on page 55 to finish. ■

"An English garden, with its orderly sections and lush blooms and growth within, is the inspiration for this design."
—Gina Gempesaw

Here's a Tip

When choosing a medium- or large-scale floral for the center of this runner, make sure that the print is dense enough so that seams don't show in the center when finished.

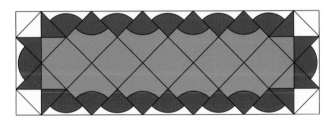

English Garden Runner
Placement Diagram 59⅜" x 19¾"

Curved Piecing

There are many traditional quilt blocks and free-form designs that use curves. Like many other quilting techniques, a few tips and a little practice will make curved piecing less of a struggle and open up your design choices.

Careful cutting and marking of curved pieces is critical to having a smooth curved seam. Curved seams are bias edges and will stretch easily without careful handling.

Curves With Templates

Make templates from template plastic or freezer paper for traditional blocks. You can also purchase acrylic templates for most common curved shapes in different sizes, or use a die-cut system to cut multiple shapes accurately.

Be sure to follow the template as closely as possible when cutting pieces. If using a rotary blade, use the smallest rotary blade size available to easily negotiate the curves. If using scissors, move the fabric/template instead of the scissors when cutting. Be sure your scissors are sharp.

Find the centers of both the convex (outer curve) and concave (inner curve) edges by folding the pieces in half; finger-press and mark with a pin. Purchased templates and die-cut pieces should have center notches. Match the centers and pin with the convex curve on the top referring to the Drunkard's Path block in Figure A.

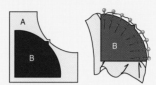

Figure A

Match and pin the seam ends. Then pin liberally between the seam ends and center, matching the seam edges and referring again to Figure A.

Slowly stitch pieces together an inch or two at a time, removing pins and keeping seam edges even.

Clip only the concave seam allowance if necessary. Press seam allowances flat toward the concave curve (Figure B).

Figure B

Over Under

Designed & Quilted by Robin Waggoner

With your own color placement and some easy paper piecing you can create a linking chain motif that can also be used in a quilt top.

Specifications
Skill Level: Intermediate
Runner Size: 46" x 14"
Block Size: 8" x 8" finished
Number of Blocks: 5

Materials
- ½ yard white solid
- ¾ yard light yellow solid
- 1 yard dark yellow solid
- Backing to size
- Batting to size
- Thread
- Basic sewing tools and supplies

Cutting

From white solid:
- Cut 1 (6" by fabric width) strip.
  Subcut strip into 5 (6") squares for piece #1.
- Cut 1 (3" by fabric width) strip.
  Subcut strip into 10 (3") squares. Cut each square in half on 1 diagonal to make 20 triangles for pieces #8–#11 for paper piecing.

From light yellow solid:
- Cut 3 (3½" by fabric width) strips for paper piecing.
- Cut 3 (3½" by fabric width) strips.
  Subcut strips into 2 (3½" x 40½") B strips and 2 (3½" x 14½") D strips.

From dark yellow solid:
- Cut 3 (3½" by fabric width) strips for paper piecing.
- Cut 3 (1" by fabric width) strips.
  Subcut strips into 2 (1" x 14½") C strips and 2 (1" x 40½") A strips.
- Cut 4 (2¼" by fabric width) binding strips.

Completing the Blocks
1. Refer to Paper-Piecing on page 38 to prepare patterns and fabric pieces for paper piecing. Paper-piecing pattern given in the pattern insert section.

2. Following instructions given in Paper-Piecing on page 38 for all piecing except begin piece #2

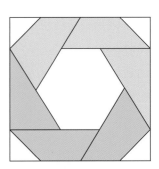

Over Under
8" x 8" Finished Block
Make 5

with a partial seam, starting stitching on the dot on the line between pieces #1 and #2 and referring to Figure 1 where the partial seam is shown in red.

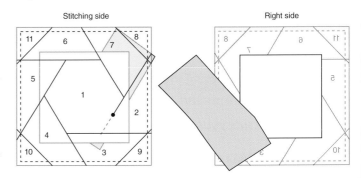

Stitching side · Right side

Figure 1

3. Continue adding pieces in numerical order until you have added pieces #7 and #8 referring to Figure 2, keeping piece #2 out of the way when stitching.

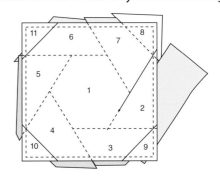

Figure 2

4. Complete stitching piece #2 in place as shown in Figure 3 to complete one Over Under block.

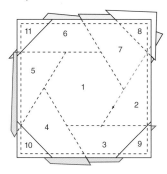

Figure 3

5. Repeat steps 2–4 to complete a total of five Over Under blocks.

Completing the Runner

1. Join the blocks to complete the runner center referring to the Assembly Diagram for positioning.

2. Remove paper and press seams open between blocks.

3. Fold and press an A strip in half wrong sides together along length. Pin the strip to the right side of a B strip matching raw edges; machine-baste to hold in place to make an A-B strip as shown in Figure 4. Repeat with the remaining A and B strips.

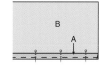

Figure 4

4. Repeat step 3 with the C and D strips, pressing the C strips in half and basting them to the D strips to make 2 C-D strips.

5. Sew the A-B strips to opposite long sides and the C-D strips to the short ends of the runner center to complete the runner top; press seams toward strips.

6. Create a quilt sandwich referring to Finishing Your Quilt on page 55.

7. Quilt as desired.

8. Bind referring to Finishing Your Quilt on page 55 to finish. ◼

"I wanted to figure out a way to do hexagons more easily. These blocks go together quickly and are very accurate." —Robin Waggoner

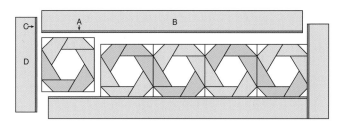

Over Under
Assembly Diagram 46" x 14"

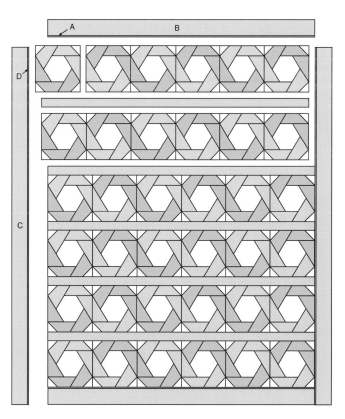

Over Under Alternate Size
Assembly Diagram 54" x 61½"
Make 36 blocks and join with 1½" finished sashing strips in 6 rows of 6 blocks each to make a lap-size quilt.

Paper-Piecing

One of the oldest quilting techniques, paper piecing allows a quilter to make blocks with odd-shaped and/or small pieces. The paper is carefully removed when the block is completed. The following instructions are for one type of paper-piecing technique; refer to a comprehensive quilting guide for other types of paper piecing.

1. Make same-size photocopies of the paper-piecing pattern given as directed on the pattern. There are several choices in regular papers as well as water-soluble papers that can be used, which are available at your local office-supply store, quilt shop or online.

2. Cut out the patterns leaving a margin around the outside bold lines as shown in Figure A. All patterns are reversed on the paper copies. Pattern color choices can be written in each numbered space on the marked side of each copy.

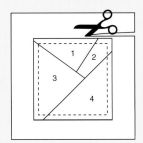

Figure A

3. When cutting fabric for paper piecing, the pieces do not have to be the exact size and shape of the area to be covered. Cut fabric pieces the general shape and ¼"–½" larger than the design area to be covered. This makes paper-piecing a good way to use up scraps.

4. With the printed side of the pattern facing you, fold along each line of the pattern as shown in Figure B, creasing the stitching lines. This will help in trimming the fabric seam allowances and in removing the paper when you are finished stitching.

Figure B

5. Turn the paper pattern over with the unmarked side facing you and position fabric indicated on pattern right side up over the space marked 1. Hold the paper up to a window or over a light box to make sure that the fabric overlaps all sides of space 1 at least ¼" as shown in Figure C from the printed side of the pattern. Pin to hold fabric in place. ***Note:*** *You can also use a light touch of glue stick. Too much glue will make the paper difficult to remove.*

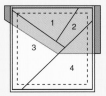

Figure C

6. Turn the paper over with the right side of the paper facing you, and fold the paper along the lines between sections 1 and 2. Trim fabric to about ¼" from the folded edge as shown in Figure D.

Figure D

7. Place the second fabric indicated right sides together with first piece. Fabric edges should be even along line between spaces 1 and 2 as shown in Figure E. Fold fabric over and check to see if second fabric piece will cover space 2.

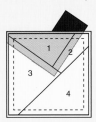

Figure E

8. With the right side of the paper facing you, hold fabric pieces together and stitch along the line between spaces 1 and 2 as shown in Figure F using a very small stitch length (18–20 stitches per inch). ***Note:*** *Using a smaller stitch length will make removing paper easier because it creates a tear line at the seam.* Always begin and end seam by sewing two to three stitches beyond the line. You do not need to backstitch. When the beginning of the seam is at the edge of the pattern, start sewing at the solid outside line of the pattern.

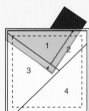

Figure F

9. Turn the pattern over, flip the second fabric back and finger-press as shown in Figure G.

Figure G

10. Continue trimming and sewing pieces in numerical order until the pattern is completely covered. Make sure pieces along the outer edge extend past the solid line to allow for a ¼" seam allowance as shown in Figure H.

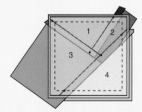

Figure H

11. When the whole block is sewn, press the block and trim all excess fabric from the block along the outside-edge solid line of paper pattern as shown in Figure I.

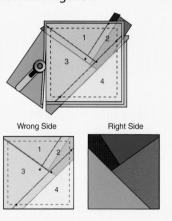

Wrong Side   Right Side

Figure I

12. After stitching blocks together, carefully remove the backing paper from completed blocks and press seams. Or, staystitch ⅛" from the outer edge of the completed block. Carefully remove backing paper and press seams. Then complete quilt top assembly.

Serene Neighborhood

Designed & Quilted by Leanna Spanner

Build your neighborhood one row at a time. This is a skill-building project that is easily adjusted in size by simply adding another block.

Project Note

Complete the blocks one type at a time, and you won't get confused or discouraged. This is a fun quilt to individualize for your own neighborhood. It would make a perfect group quilt—have each person make a type of block or one of each block in his or her own personal colors.

Specifications

Skill Level: Confident Beginner
Quilt Size: 60" x 72½"
Block Sizes: 10" x 10" finished and 10" x 12½" finished
Number of Blocks: 36 and 6

Materials

See individual block construction for list of materials for each block type. The following list of materials is needed to complete the quilt after the blocks are pieced.

- ⅝ yard blue tonal
- Backing to size
- Batting to size
- Thread
- Basic sewing tools and supplies

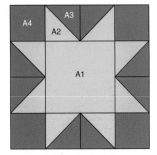

Star
10" x 10" Finished Block
Make 6

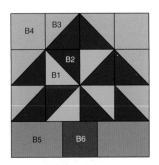

Tree
10" x 10" Finished Block
Make 6

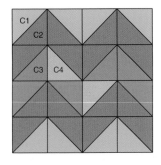

Stream
10" x 10" Finished Block
Make 6

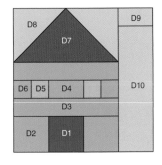

House
10" x 10" Finished Block
Make 6

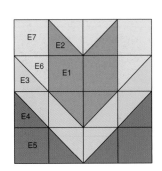

Tulip
10" x 10" Finished Block
Make 6

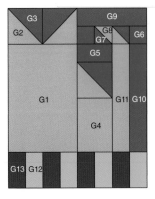

Cat
10" x 12½" Finished Block
Make 6

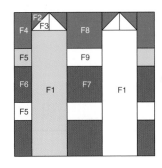

Picket Fence
10" x 10" Finished Block
Make 6

Cutting

From blue tonal:
• Cut 7 (2¼" by fabric width) binding strips.

Star Blocks

Materials
• ½ yard pale yellow plaid (stars)
• ½ yard dark blue tonal (sky)

Cutting

From pale yellow plaid:
• Cut 1 (5½" by fabric width) strip.
  Subcut strip into 6 (5½") A1 squares.
• Cut 2 (3⅜" by fabric width) strips.
  Subcut strips into 24 (3⅜") A2 squares.

From dark blue tonal:
• Cut 2 (3⅜" by fabric width) strips.
  Subcut strips into 24 (3⅜") A3 squares.
• Cut 2 (3" by fabric width) strips.
  Subcut strips into 24 (3") A4 squares.

Completing the Star Blocks

1. Draw a diagonal line from corner to corner on the wrong side of each A2 square.

2. Referring to Figure 1, place an A2 square right sides together with an A3 square and stitch ¼" on each side of the marked line. Cut apart on the marked line and press open with seam toward A3 to complete two A2-A3 units. Repeat to make a total of 48 A2-A3 units.

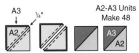

Figure 1

3. To complete one Star block, select one A1 square, eight A2-A3 units and four A4 squares.

4. Join two A2-A3 units to make a side unit as shown in Figure 2; press seam open. Repeat to make a total of four side units.

Figure 2   **Figure 3**

5. Sew a side unit to opposite sides of the A1 square to make the center row as shown in Figure 3; press seams toward A1.

6. Sew an A4 square to opposite ends of each remaining side unit to make the top and bottom rows referring to Figure 4; press seams toward A4 squares.

Figure 4

7. Sew the top and bottom rows to the center row to complete one Star block referring to Figure 5; press seams toward the center row.

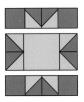

Figure 5

8. Repeat steps 3–7 to complete a total of six Star blocks, pressing seams of three blocks away from the center row.

Tree Blocks

Materials
• 1 fat quarter each:
  brown tonal (trunks)
  pinecone print (pinwheel)
  medium green tonal (grass)
  dark green tonal (trees)
• ½ yard medium blue tonal (sky)

Cutting

From brown tonal:
• Cut 1 (3" x 21") strip.
  Subcut strip into 6 (3") B6 squares.

From pinecone print:
• Cut 2 (3⅜" x 21") strips.
  Subcut strips into 12 (3⅜") B1 squares.

From medium green tonal:
• Cut 2 (4¼" x 21") strips.
  Subcut strips into 12 (3" x 4¼") B5 rectangles.

From dark green tonal:
• Cut 5 (3⅜" x 21") strips.
  Subcut strips into 30 (3⅜") B2 squares.

From medium blue tonal:
• Cut 1 (3" by fabric width) strip.
  Subcut strip into 12 (3") B4 squares.

- Cut 2 (3⅜" by fabric width) strips.
  Subcut strips into 18 (3⅜") B3 squares.

Completing the Tree Blocks

1. Draw a diagonal line from corner to corner on the wrong side of each B1 and B3 square.

2. Referring to Figure 6, place a B1 square right sides together with a B2 square and stitch ¼" on each side of the marked line. Cut apart on the marked line and press open with seam toward B2 to complete two B1-B2 units. Repeat to make a total of 24 B1-B2 units.

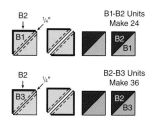

Figure 6

3. Repeat step 2 with B2 and B3 squares to make a total of 36 B2-B3 units, again referring to Figure 6.

4. To complete one Tree block, select one B6 square, two B5 rectangles, two B4 squares, four B1-B2 units and six B2-B3 units.

5. Sew B5 to opposite sides of B6 to make the trunk unit referring to Figure 7; press seams toward B5 rectangles.

Figure 7

6. Arrange and join the remaining pieced units in rows with the B4 squares referring to Figure 8 for positioning; press seams in adjacent rows in opposite directions.

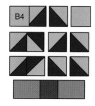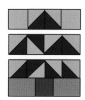

Figure 8   **Figure 9**

7. Join the rows referring to Figure 9 to complete one Tree block; press.

8. Repeat steps 4–7 to complete a total of six Tree blocks, pressing rows of three blocks in one direction and three in the opposite direction.

Stream Blocks

Materials
- 1 fat quarter each:
  blue duck print (water)
  blue tonal (water)
  green print (grass)
- ½ yard tan print (soil)

Cutting

From blue duck print:
- Cut 1 (3⅜" x 21") strip.
  Subcut strip into 6 (3⅜") C4 squares.

From blue tonal:
- Cut 3 (3⅜" x 21") strips.
  Subcut strips into 18 (3⅜") C3 squares.

From green print:
- Cut 4 (3⅜" x 21") strips.
  Subcut strips into 24 (3⅜") C1 squares.

From tan print:
- Cut 4 (3⅜" by fabric width) strips.
  Subcut strips into 48 (3⅜") C2 squares.

Completing the Stream Blocks

1. Draw a diagonal line from corner to corner on the wrong side of each C2 square.

2. Referring to Figure 10, place a C2 square right sides together with a C1 square and stitch ¼" on each side of the marked line. Cut apart on the marked line and press open with seam toward C2 to complete two C1-C2 units. Repeat to make a total of 48 C1-C2 units.

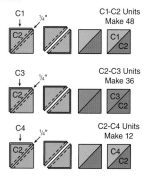

Figure 10

3. Repeat step 2 with C2 and C3 squares to make 36 C2-C3 units, again referring to Figure 10.

4. Repeat step 2 with C2 and C4 squares to make 12 C2-C4 units, again referring to Figure 10.

5. To complete one Stream block, select eight C1-C2 units, six C2-C3 units and two C2-C4 units.

6. Arrange and join the pieced units in four rows of four units each referring to Figure 11 for positioning; press seams in adjacent rows in opposite directions. ***Note:*** *The C2-C4 units were placed randomly in each block in the sample quilt.*

Figure 11

7. Join the rows as pieced to complete one Stream block, again referring to Figure 11; press seams in one direction.

8. Repeat steps 5–7 to complete a total of six Stream blocks, pressing rows of three blocks in one direction and three in the opposite direction.

House Blocks

Materials
- 1 fat quarter each:
   gold print (windows)
   tan brick print (chimneys)
   light blue tonal (sky)
- 6 dark print/tonal fat quarters for roof and door pieces (1 for each house)
- 6 light or medium print/tonal fat quarters for house pieces (1 for each house)

Cutting

From gold print:
- Cut 1 (1¾" x 21") strip.
   Subcut strip into 12 (1¾") D5 squares.

From tan brick print:
- Cut 1 (9¼" x 21") strip.
   Subcut strip into 6 (3" x 9¼") D10 rectangles.

From light blue tonal:
- Cut 3 (4¼" x 21") strips.
   Subcut strips into 12 (4¼") D8 squares.
- Cut 1 (1¾" x 21") strip.
   Subcut strip into 6 (1¾" x 3") D9 rectangles.

From each dark print/tonal fat quarter:
- Cut 1 (4¼" x 8") D7 rectangle and 1 (3") D1 square.

From each light/medium print/tonal fat quarter:
- Cut 2 (1¾" x 21") strips.
   Subcut strips into 2 (1¾" x 8") D3 strips, 2 (1¾") D6 squares and 1 (1¾" x 3") D4 rectangle.
- Cut 1 (3" x 21") strip.
   Subcut strip into 2 (3") D2 squares.

Completing the House Blocks

1. Draw a diagonal line from corner to corner on the wrong side of each D8 square.

2. To piece one House block, select one each same-fabric D1 square and D7 rectangle, two D5 squares, and two each same-fabric D2, D3 and D6 pieces and one D4 piece to match. Select two marked D8 squares and one each D9 and D10 piece.

3. Sew a D1 square between two D2 squares to make the door unit referring to Figure 12; press seams toward D1.

Figure 12

4. Sew a D5 square to a D6 square; repeat. Sew these units to opposite sides of the D4 rectangle to make the window unit as shown in Figure 13; press seams toward D5.

Figure 13

5. Referring to Figure 14, place a D8 square on one end of the D7 rectangle and stitch on the marked line; trim seam to ¼" and press D8 to the right side. Repeat on the opposite end of D7 to complete the roof unit.

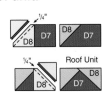

Figure 14   **Figure 15**

6. Sew a D3 strip to opposite sides of the window unit and add the door unit and the roof unit to complete the house unit as shown in Figure 15; press seams toward D3 strips.

7. Sew the D9 rectangle to the D10 rectangle to complete the chimney unit; press.

8. Sew the chimney unit to the right edge of the house unit to complete the House block as shown in Figure 16; press seam toward the chimney unit.

Figure 16

9. Repeat steps 2–8 to complete a total of six House blocks.

Tulip Blocks

Materials
- 1 fat quarter each:
  blue print (sky)
  white-with-green leaf print (leaves)
  dark green print (ground)
- 6 tonal fat quarters (1 for each tulip)

Cutting

From blue print:
- Cut 2 (3⅜" x 21") strips.
  Subcut strips into 12 (3⅜") E6 squares.
- Cut 2 (3" x 21") strips.
  Subcut strips into 12 (3") E7 squares.

From white-with-green leaf print:
- Cut 4 (3⅜" x 21") strips.
  Subcut strips into 24 (3⅜") E3 squares.

From dark green print:
- Cut 2 (3⅜" x 21") strips.
  Subcut strips into 12 (3⅜") E4 squares.
- Cut 2 (3" x 21") strips.
  Subcut strips into 12 (3") E5 squares.

From each tonal fat quarter:
- Cut 1 (3⅜" x 21") strip.
  Subcut strip into 2 (3⅜") E2 squares and
    2 (3") E1 squares.

Completing the Tulip Blocks
1. Draw a diagonal line from corner to corner on the wrong side of each E3 and six E6 squares.

2. Referring to Figure 17, place an E3 square right sides together with an E4 square and stitch ¼" on each side of the marked line. Cut apart on the marked line and press open with seam toward E4 to complete two E3-E4 units. Repeat to make a total of 24 E3-E4 units.

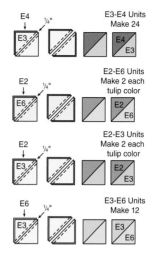

Figure 17

3. Referring again to Figure 17, repeat step 2 with E2 and E6 squares, and with E2 and E3 squares to make two each E2-E6 and E2-E3 units each tulip color; repeat step 2 with E3 and E6 squares to make 12 E3-E6 units.

4. To complete one block, select two each E7 and E5 squares, two each same-fabric E1 squares and E2-E6 and E2-E3 units, two E3-E6 units and four E3-E4 units.

5. Arrange and join the pieced units with the E1, E5 and E7 squares in rows referring to Figure 18; press seams in adjacent rows in opposite directions.

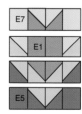

Figure 18

6. Join the rows as pieced to complete one Tulip block; press seams in one direction.

7. Repeat steps 4–6 to complete a total of six different-color Tulip blocks, pressing rows of three blocks in one direction and three in the opposite direction.

Picket Fence Blocks

Materials
- 1 fat quarter each:
  blue tonal (sky)
  green print (grass)
  white tonal (fence)
  white-with-green leaf print (fence)

Cutting

From blue tonal:
- Cut 2 (2⅛" x 21") strips.
  Subcut strips into 12 (2⅛") F2 squares.
- Cut 2 (1¾" x 21") strips.
  Subcut strips into 12 (1¾" x 3") F4 rectangles.
- Cut 1 (3" x 21") strip.
  Subcut strip into 6 (3") F8 squares.

From green print:
- Cut 4 (3" x 21") strips.
  Subcut strips into 12 (3") F7 squares and
    24 (1¾" x 3") F6 rectangles.

From white tonal:
- Cut 2 (2⅛" x 21") strips.
  Subcut strips into 12 (2⅛") F3 squares.
- Cut 1 (9¼" x 21") strip.
  Subcut strip into 6 (3" x 9¼") F1 rectangles.
- Cut 2 (1¾" x 21") strips.
  Subcut strips into 12 (1¾") F5 squares and
    7 (1¾" x 3") F9 rectangles.

From white-with-green leaf print:
- Cut 2 (1¾" x 21") strips.
  Subcut strips into 12 (1¾") F5 squares and
    5 (1¾" x 3") F9 rectangles.
- Cut 1 (9¼" x 21") strip.
  Subcut strip into 6 (3" x 9¼") F1 rectangles.

Completing the Picket Fence Blocks
These blocks are mixed and matched to make six variations of the block with placement of the white tonal and white-with-green leaf pieces moved around. One block has two F1 print fence posts instead of one tonal and one print. The F5 squares and the F9 rectangles are also moved around within the blocks. The cutting list includes pieces to make the blocks shown in the sample quilt.

1. Mark a diagonal line from corner to corner on the wrong side of each F3 square.

2. Referring to Figure 19, place an F3 square right sides together with an F2 square and stitch ¼" on each side of the marked line. Cut apart on the marked line to make two F2-F3 units. Repeat to make a total of 24 units.

Figure 19

3. To complete one block, select the following: one F8 square; two each F1, F4, F7 and F9 pieces; and four each F2-F3 units, F5 and F6 pieces.

4. Sew an F5 square between two F6 rectangles and add an F5 square and an F4 rectangle to make one side unit as shown in Figure 20; press seams in one direction. Repeat to make a second side unit.

Side Unit
Make 2

Figure 20

5. Join two F2-F3 units and sew to F1 to make a fence post unit as shown in Figure 21; press. Repeat to make a second fence post unit.

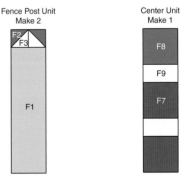

Fence Post Unit
Make 2

Center Unit
Make 1

Figure 21   **Figure 22**

6. Join two F7 squares with two F9 rectangles and one F8 square to make the center unit as shown in Figure 22; press seams in one direction.

7. Arrange and join the side units with the fence post units and the center unit to make a Picket Fence block as shown in Figure 23; press seams toward the fence post units.

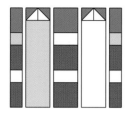

Figure 23

8. Repeat steps 3–7 to complete a total of six Picket Fence blocks, press seams in three blocks in one direction and three blocks in the opposite direction. *Note: Figure 24 shows the block variations used in the sample quilt.*

Make 1 of each

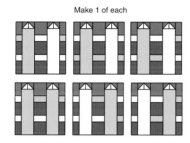

Figure 24

Cat Blocks

Materials
- 1 fat quarter each 6 different prints (cats)
- ¼ yard light green tonal (grass)
- ¼ yard dark green tonal (grass)
- ½ yard blue tonal (sky)

Cutting

From each print fat quarter:
- Cut 1 (8" x 21") strip.
  Subcut strip into 1 (5½" x 8") G1 rectangle, 1 (1¾" x 8") G11 rectangle and 2 (3⅜") G2 squares.
- Cut 1 (3" x 21") strip.
  Subcut strip into 1 (3" x 4¼") G4 rectangle and 1 (2⅛") G8 square.

From light green tonal:
- Cut 2 (1¾" by fabric width) G12 strips.

From dark green tonal:
- Cut 2 (1¾" by fabric width) G13 strips.

From blue tonal:
- Cut 1 (8" by fabric width) strip.
  Subcut strip into 6 (1¾" x 8") G10 rectangles, 6 (1¾" x 5½") G9 rectangles, 6 (1¾" x 3") G5 rectangles, 12 (1¾") G6 squares and 6 (2⅛") G7 squares.
- Cut 1 (3⅜" by fabric width) strip.
  Subcut strip into 12 (3⅜") G3 squares.

Completing the Cat Blocks
1. Mark a diagonal line from corner to corner on the wrong side of each G2 and G8 square.

2. Referring to Figure 25, place a G2 square right sides together with a G3 square and stitch ¼" on each side of the marked line. Cut apart on the marked line and press open with seam toward G3 to complete two G2-G3 units. Repeat with remaining G2 and G3 squares to make a total of four G2-G3 units in each cat print. Set aside one unit of each print for another project.

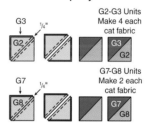

Figure 25

3. Repeat step 2 with the G7 and G8 squares to make two G7-G8 units from each cat print, again referring to Figure 25.

4. Sew a G12 strip to a G13 strip with right sides together along length to make a grass strip set; press seam toward G13. Repeat to make a second grass strip set.

5. Subcut the grass strip sets into 24 (3" x 3") grass units as shown in Figure 26.

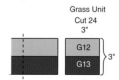

Figure 26

6. Select 1 each same-fabric G1, G4 and G11 piece, two same-fabric G7-G8 units, three same-fabric G2-G3 units, two G6 squares, one each G5, G9 and G10 piece, and four grass units.

7. Join two G2-G3 units; press seam open. Sew to the G1 rectangle to make the front unit as shown in Figure 27; press seam toward G1.

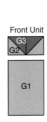

Front Unit
Figure 27

Back Unit
Figure 28

8. Sew a G2-G3 unit to G4 and add G5; press seams toward G4 and G5. Sew a G6 square to a G7-G8 unit and sew to the G5 side of the pieced unit to complete the back unit as shown in Figure 28; press seam toward G6 and then G5.

9. Sew a G7-G8 unit to G11; press seam toward G11. Sew a G6 square to G10; press seam toward G6. Join the pieced strips to make the tail section as shown in Figure 29; press seam toward G6-G10.

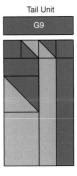

Tail Section
Figure 29

Tail Unit
Figure 30

10. Sew the tail section to the back unit and add G9 to the top to complete the tail unit as shown in Figure 30; press seam toward the tail section and then G9.

11. Join the front unit and the tail unit to complete the cat unit as shown in Figure 31; press seam toward the front unit.

Figure 31

Here's a Tip

Press seams of half of the blocks for one row in one direction and half in the opposite direction so that the seams will lock together when joined to make a row referring to Figure A.

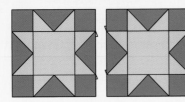

Figure A

12. Join four grass units to make a grass strip; press seams in one direction. Sew the grass strip to the bottom of the cat unit to complete the Cat block referring to Figure 32.

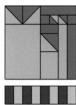

Figure 32

13. Repeat steps 6–12 to complete a total of six Cat blocks, each using a different print for the cat shapes in the blocks.

Completing the Quilt

1. Arrange and join the blocks in seven rows with six same-pattern blocks in each row referring to the Assembly Diagram; press seams in adjacent rows in opposite directions.

2. Join the rows to complete the quilt top; press.

3. Create a quilt sandwich referring to Finishing Your Quilt on page 55.

4. Quilt as desired.

5. Bind referring to Finishing Your Quilt on page 55 to finish. ∎

"My goal was to create a landscape-type scene. The top starts with the stars in the sky just before dawn. Row 2 moves to trees in the woods, then on to the stream running through the woods. Next we come to the homestead with a flower garden in front of the house. Finishing the scene is the country picket fence and family cats sitting in the grass." —Leanna Spanner

Serene Neighborhood
Assembly Diagram 60" x 72½"

Serene Neighborhood Alternate Size
Assembly Diagram 60" x 82½"
Add another pieced row to make a longer quilt.

Thomas Goes Fishing

Design by Claire Haillot
Quilted by Colleen Paul

This quilt gives you two options for a unique paper-pieced row. Take Thomas fishing or create a walk through your garden. This is an opportunity to design with a border fabric or a large-scale fabric.

Specifications
Skill Level: Intermediate
Quilt Size: 62" x 98"
Block Size: 8" x 8" finished
Number of Blocks: 16

Materials
- ¾ yard coordinating stripe
- 1 yard black solid
- 1⅛ yards fish print
- 1½ yards total assorted print and solid scraps
- 2 yards fish border print
- 3¼ yards blue bubble print
- Backing to size
- Batting to size
- Thread
- Basic sewing tools and supplies

Cutting
Refer to the Block and Assembly Diagrams for color suggestions for each block.

Refer to Paper-Piecing on page 38 for cutting and piecing instructions to make the paper-pieced blocks.

This pattern was written for use with a border print. Refer to Using Border Prints on page 53 for tips. If a border print is not available, substitute the fish print or other appropriate prints or solids for fish border print.

From coordinating stripe:
- Cut 8 (2¼" by fabric width) binding strips.

From fish print:
- Cut 4 (8½" by fabric width) G strips.

From fish border print:
- Cut 1 (15½" x 62½") D strip along length.
- Cut 2 (7" x 62½") E strips along length.
- Cut 2 (3½" x 62½") F strips along length.

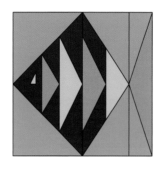

Fish 1
8" x 8" Finished Block
Make 4

Fish 1 (tail option)
8" x 8" Finished Block
Make 4

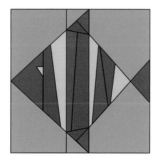

Fish 2
8" x 8" Finished Block
Make 2

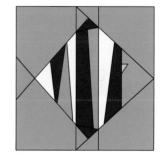

Fish 2 Reversed
8" x 8" Finished Block
Make 2

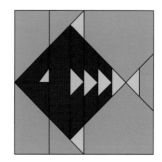

Fish 3
8" x 8" Finished Block
Make 3

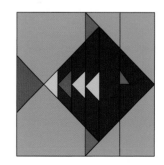

Fish 3 (tail option)
8" x 8" Finished Block
Make 1

From blue bubble print:
- Cut 8 (2½" x 62½") C strips and 2 (8½" x 70") A/B strips along the length of the fabric.
- Prepare template for Fish 3 H background pattern and cut as directed.

Completing the Fish Blocks

1. Refer to Paper-Piecing on page 38 to prepare patterns given in the pattern insert and fabric pieces for paper piecing and piecing techniques.

2. Piece four each Fish 1 and Fish 1 (tail option), two each Fish 2 and Fish 2 Reversed, three Fish 3 and one Fish 3 (tail option) to complete a total of 16 fish blocks. *Note: Join sections to make complete optional tail sections for four Fish 1 and one Fish 3 as shown in Figure 1.*

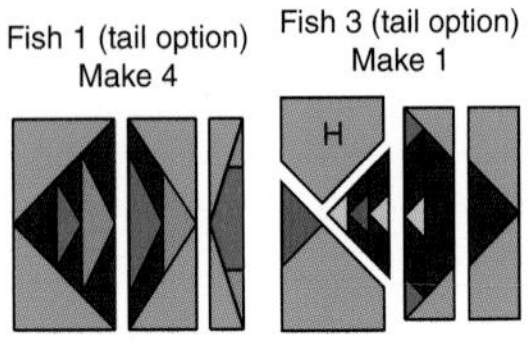

Fish 1 (tail option)   Fish 3 (tail option)
Make 4   Make 1

Figure 1

Completing the Quilt

1. Select and arrange four fish together in a row with fish facing to the left. Add eyes to the fish as shown in the sample, using appliqué eyes cut from scraps, embroidery or buttons as desired.

2. Cut seven 1½"–2" x 8½" A sashing strips from one A/B strip to sew between the blocks. Repeat to cut seven more A sashing strips from the second A/B strip.

3. Join four Fish blocks with A sashing strips to make a pieced strip as shown in Figure 2 or referring to the Assembly Diagram for variety of placement and strip widths; press seams toward the A strips. *Note: Two rows use three A sashing strips, and two rows use four A sashing strips in sample.*

Figure 2

4. Measure the pieced strip from step 3. Subtract this amount from 62½" and cut a B strip this length plus 1"–2" for safety from remainder of one A/B

strip. Sew B to the pieced strip to complete a fish row as shown in Figure 3; press seam toward B. Trim the fish row to 8½" x 62½".

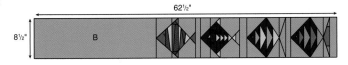

Figure 3

5. Repeat steps 3 and 4 to make four fish rows referring to the Assembly Diagram for positioning of the fish blocks in the rows. *Note: Create left- and right-facing fish rows by turning the symmetrical Fish 1 and 3 blocks to face either direction and adding Fish 2 Reversed blocks to right-facing rows.*

6. Sew a C strip to opposite long sides of each fish row; press seams toward C strips.

7. Referring to the Assembly Diagram, arrange and join the bordered fish rows with the D, E and F strips; press seams away from the fish rows.

8. Join the G strips on the short ends to make one long strip; press. Subcut strip into two 6½" x 62½" G strips.

9. Create a quilt sandwich referring to Finishing Your Quilt on page 55.

10. Quilt as desired.

11. Bind referring to Finishing Your Quilt on page 55 to finish. ■

"I loved the fabric and wanted to feature it on the center of the bed instead of around it as a border, so I came up with four paper-pieced fish to embellish it." —Claire Haillot

Here's a Tip

The Add-A-Quarter Ruler makes it easy to add the ¼" seam allowance when cutting all the little pieces used in the paper piecing.

Using Border Prints

The size of your border print may vary from the sizes given. Because fill-in pieces are added to make the rows, the only constant in this quilt is the size of the blocks. The length of the strips used to join the blocks into rows and the width of the strips to join those rows can all be different. This makes it easy to make a quilt in a size to fit its use, whether it will be on a bed or a wall. Decide on the finished length and width, and use those measurements to build your quilt.

Pay attention to print orientation when buying fabric. Most border prints are printed along the length of the fabric, while most directional prints are printed across the width of the fabric. In the sample quilt, the top and bottom borders are cut from a directional fish print that was printed across the width, so strips must be cut across the fabric width and joined to make the required strip lengths.

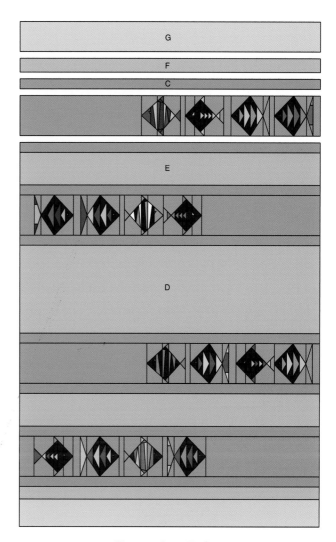

Thomas Goes Fishing
Assembly Diagram 62" x 96"

Flower Row

If you are not interested in making the playful children's quilt shown for Thomas Goes Fishing, substitute a flower-design block for the fish-design blocks using the paper-piecing patterns given on the pattern insert. You will need four stitched units of each pattern to complete one block. The sample shown features an Orange Flower block with orange petals and a purple center, and a Purple Flower block with purple petals and an orange center.

The rows are pieced in a similar manner to the Thomas Goes Fishing rows with sashing pieces sized to your preference and a larger strip on one end to make the row as wide as you want it to be.

Design your own row quilt with blocks made using this easy paper-pieced design; then you will have your own colorful flower garden inside any time of the year.

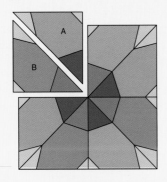

Orange Flower
8" x 8" Finished Block
Make 2

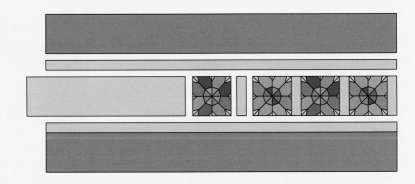

Flower Row
Assembly Diagram 62" x 28"

Finishing Your Quilt

1. Press quilt top on both sides; check for proper seam pressing and trim all loose threads.

2. Sandwich batting between the stitched top and the prepared backing piece; pin or baste layers together to hold. Mark quilting design and quilt as desired by hand or machine.

3. When quilting is complete, remove pins or basting. Trim batting and backing fabric edges even with raw edges of quilt top.

4. Join binding strips on short ends with diagonal seams to make one long strip; trim seams to ¼" and press seams open.

5. Fold the binding strip in half with wrong sides together along length; press.

6. Sew binding to quilt edges, matching raw edges, mitering corners and overlapping ends.

7. Fold binding to the back side and stitch in place to finish.

Special Thanks

Please join us in thanking the talented designers whose work is featured in this collection.

Gina Gempesaw
English Garden Runner, page 31
Quick Snaps, page 3

Claire Haillot
Thomas Goes Fishing, page 51

Nancy Scott
Hanging by a Chain, page 16

Wendy Sheppard
Stardom, page 10

Leanna Spanner
Serene Neighborhood, page 40

Robin Waggoner
Over Under, page 34
Ribbon Play, page 25

Julie Weaver
Abacus, page 6
Evening Blooms Bed Runner, page 21

Supplies

We would like to thank the following manufacturers who provided materials to our designers to make sample projects for this book.

Abacus, page 6: Thermore batting from Hobbs.

Stardom, page 10: Concerto fabric collection by Kanvas for Benartex; Tuscany Silk batting from Hobbs; Mako 50 cotton thread from Aurifil used to make sample.

Hanging by a Chain, page 16: Krystal fabric collection from Michael Miller Fabric and TK Quilting and Design digital quilting patterns (www.tkquilting.com) used to make sample.

Evening Blooms Bed Runner, page 21: Evening Blooms fabric collection from Riley Blake Designs and Warm & Natural cotton batting from The Warm Company used to make sample.

Serene Neighborhood, page 40: Nature-Fil Bamboo batting from Fairfield and Quilting With Antique Lace Pantograph by Urban Elementz.

Annie's® Row Quilts: Longitudes & Latitudes is published by Annie's, 306 East Parr Road, Berne, IN 46711. Printed in USA. Copyright © 2014 Annie's. All rights reserved. This publication may not be reproduced in part or in whole without written permission from the publisher.

RETAIL STORES: If you would like to carry this pattern book or any other Annie's publication, visit AnniesWSL.com.

Every effort has been made to ensure that the instructions in this pattern book are complete and accurate. We cannot, however, take responsibility for human error, typographical mistakes or variations in individual work. Please visit AnniesCustomerService.com to check for pattern updates.

ISBN: 978-1-57367-381-5
3 4 5 6 7 8 9